DATE DUE

2/7/08	
RENEWALS	
847-362-0438	
www.cooklib.org	

The Library Store   #47-0106

POLAR
Habitats

By **Barbara Taylor**

GARETH**STEVENS**
GS
P U B L I S H I N G
A Member of the WRC Media Family of Companies

Please visit our web site at: www.garethstevens.com
For a free color catalog describing Gareth Stevens Publishing's
list of high-quality books and multimedia programs,
call 1-800-542-2595 or 1-800-387-3178 (Canada).
Gareth Stevens Publishing's fax: (414) 332-3567.

Library of Congress Cataloging-in-Publication Data

Taylor, Barbara, 1954-
  Polar habitats / Barbara Taylor. – North American ed.
      p. cm. — (Exploring habitats)
  Includes bibliographical references and index.
  ISBN-10: 0-8368-7256-8 – ISBN-13: 978-0-8368-7256-9 (lib. bdg.)
  1. Polar regions—Juvenile literature. I. Title. II. Series.
QH84.1.T39   2006
578.75'86—dc22   2006044330

This North American edition first published in 2007 by
Gareth Stevens Publishing
A Member of the WRC Media Family of Companies
330 West Olive Street, Suite 100
Milwaukee, WI 53212 USA

This U.S. edition copyright © 2007 by Gareth Stevens, Inc. Original
edition copyright © 2002 by ticktock Entertainment Ltd. First published
in Great Britain in 1999 by ticktock Publishing Ltd., Unit 2, Orchard
Business Centre, North Farm Road, Tunbridge Wells, Kent, TN2 3XF.

Gareth Stevens editor: Richard Hantula
Gareth Stevens designer: Charlie Dahl
Gareth Stevens managing editor: Mark J.Sachner
Gareth Stevens art direction: Tammy West
Gareth Stevens production: Jessica Morris

Picture Credits: t=top, b=bottom, c=centre, l=left, r=right, OFC=outside
front cover, OBC=outside back cover, IFC=inside front cover

AKG Photo; 3rb. B&C Alexander Photography; 2l, 2c, 2/3t, 3tl, 4tl, 4/5
(main pic), 5c, 6tl, 7br, 7bl, 8bl, 8/9b, 8/9c, 9br, 10bl, 10tl, 10cr, 12/13b + 32,
12/13c, 14/15 (main pic), 15tr, 15cr, 16l, 18br, 18cl, 18tc, 18/19t, 22tl,
22/23b, 23c, 23tr, 24tl, 24c, 25cr, 25tl, 25/26 (main pic), 25/26c, 26tr, 28bc,
28bl, 28tl, 29bl, 29br, 29c, 29tl, 30l, 30/31bc, 31cl, 31tr. Oxford Scientific
Films; 3tr, 5tr, 6tr, 8c, 8l, 11r, 11tl, 13br, 14/15c, 16c, 18cr, 19tc, 20tl, 21br,
21tr, 21tl, 21rc, 24bl, 24/25c, 25tr, 31br. Planet Earth Pictures; IFC, 3cl, 9tl,
9tr, 10/11c, 12t, 12b, 13tr, 13rc, 14tl, 16/17b, 17cl, 17tl, 17tr, 19b, 20/21c,
20/21b, 23tl, 30cl. Survival Anglia; 12c.

Every effort has been made to trace the copyright holders and we apologize in
advance for any unintentional omissions. We would be pleased to insert the
appropriate acknowledgement in any subsequent edition of this publication.

Printed in the United States of America

1 2 3 4 5 6 7 8 9 10 09 08 07 06

CONTENTS

Pole to Pole   4-5

Weather and Climate   6-7

The North Pole/
   The South Pole   8-9

Polar Plants   10-11

Arctic Animals   12-13

Antarctic Animals   14-15

Surviving the Cold   16-17

Animals on the Move   18-19

Predators and Prey   20-21

Defense   22-23

Courtship   24-25

Nests, Eggs, and Young   26-27

Living Together   28-29

People at the Poles   30-31

Protecting the Poles   32-33

For Further Information   34

Glossary   35

Index   36

COLD SURVIVAL

The Arctic fox is one of the few permanent residents of the Arctic. This hardy, resourceful animal is able to survive harsh winter conditions, unlike the region's many summer visitors.

Wild, icy cold, and spectacularly beautiful, the polar regions extend for over 1,600 miles (2,600 kilometers) in all directions around the North Pole and the South Pole. They are the last two wilderness areas on Earth. A vast area of frozen ocean, the Arctic Ocean, surrounds the North Pole, while the South Pole is surrounded by a frozen continent called Antarctica. Antarctica is the fifth largest continent and has 90 percent of all the ice on Earth. Both the Arctic and the Antarctic have long, dark winters, when the Sun never shines. During the short, cool summers the Sun never sets, and many animals visit polar lands to feed, nest, and raise their young. Only a few especially hardy animals manage to live in the Arctic and Antarctic all year around.

ARCTIC TRAVEL

The harsh terrain and the savage and unpredictable climate of the polar regions combine to make travel dangerous and exhausting. In the Arctic, native peoples originally used long, low sleds pulled by huskies – sturdy, fast dogs presumably bred from from Arctic wolves – to transport heavy loads (*left and above*). Today's huskies are of a variety of breeds, but as in bygone times, they are hardy, strong, and intelligent and work in a strict hierarchy under a lead dog. Dogsleds remain one of the best ways to travel in polar regions, but most transportation there is now motorized and includes vehicles such as snowmobiles.

FROM POLE TO POLE

The graceful and elegant Arctic tern (*right*) flies from the top of the world to the bottom and back again every year – a round trip of some 25,000 miles (40,000 km). It flies farther than any other bird, in order to spend summer in both the Arctic and the Antarctic. The Arctic tern probably experiences more hours of daylight than any other creature on Earth.

ICY PENGUINS

Several species of penguin (*left*) live and breed in south polar regions. The penguins shown *above* are resting on a rare blue iceberg.

CHANGING CLIMATES

Dawn redwood fossils dating back 100 million years have been found in the Arctic.

The poles have not always been so cold. Ice has built up at the poles only during the last 30 million or so years, and the lands around the Arctic and under the Antarctic ice have been in their current positions for less than 50 million years. The continent of Antarctica was probably once near the Equator, where the climate was warmer and subtropical. Ferns, cycads, trees, and other green plants grew there, and dinosaurs roamed the land. We know little about the prehistoric origins of the Arctic region, but it is clear that landmasses have drifted slowly about and sea levels have changed. This has sometimes allowed land bridges to form between continents such as Asia and North America, along which animals could migrate.

Fierce dinosaurs resembling this Allosaurus once lived in the Antarctic.

NORTH

THE POLES TODAY

The geographic poles are at opposite ends of the globe, marking the points that are farthest north and farthest south (*left*). A magnetic pole lies near each of the geographic poles, but the magnetic poles are always moving. Compasses use a magnetic needle, so they point to magnetic north and south rather than to the geographic poles.

SOUTH

WEATHER AND CLIMATE

BLIZZARD WINDS

Strong winds draw heat away from the body and make animals very cold. Sitting curled up with its back to the wind, this husky (*above*) is trying to expose as little of its body as possible to the freezing wind. Its thick fur helps to keep it warm.

Polar climates are intensely cold and dry, with very strong winds. Cold air moves from the poles toward the Equator, helping to keep the Earth from getting too hot. Antarctica is the coldest and windiest place on Earth. Average temperatures in the interior fall below -76 °Fahrenheit (-60 °Celsius) in the winter. The roaring, ferocious winds – speeds of up to 200 miles (320 km) per hour – produce blizzards and snowdrifts. An unprotected person could freeze solid in minutes. Both polar regions are cold deserts, since most areas receive less than 10 inches (240 millimeters) of rain or snow a year.

Yet four-fifths of the world's freshwater lies in the ice sheets on Antarctica and Greenland. Polar regions have only two seasons, summer and winter. When it is summer in the Arctic, it is winter in the Antarctic, and vice versa. Summer brings 24 hours of daylight, with the Sun still shining in the sky at midnight, and so the polar regions are sometimes called "lands of the midnight Sun."

ARCTIC SUMMER

Caribou (also called reindeer) visit Arctic lands in summer when the top layer of the ground thaws and there are plenty of plants for them to eat (*right*). Unfortunately for them, clouds of midges, gnats, and mosquitoes also swarm over the marshy ground in summer. The insects are, however, useful food for some of the birds that visit the Arctic for the summer season.

CURTAINS OF LIGHT

Glowing, shimmering curtains of light called auroras sometimes appear in polar skies *(left)*, especially near the magnetic poles. They occur because the Earth's magnetic poles attract charged particles given off by the Sun. When these particles strike gas particles in the Earth's atmosphere, colored light is produced. The display is called the Aurora Borealis, or Northern Lights, in the Arctic and the Aurora Australis, or Southern Lights, in the Antarctic. Auroras are difficult to photograph because they are very faint and move rapidly.

WHY ARE THE POLES COLD?

The Sun's rays bring heat and light to the Earth. The Earth, however, is curved like a ball, so the Sun's rays are weaker and more spread out at the poles than at the Equator (*right*). The rays also have to travel farther through the atmosphere to reach the poles, and the atmosphere absorbs much of the heat, making the poles colder. The white ice and snow at the poles reflect back between 50 and 90 percent of the Sun's heat, making the poles colder still.

BERING STRAIT

CANADA

ARCTIC CIRCLE

ARCTIC

ARCTIC OCEAN

RUSSIA

NORTH POLE

BAFFIN BAY

BARENTS SEA

GREENLAND

NORWEGIAN SEA

FINLAND

ICELAND

THE NORTH POLE

Although the areas around the North Pole and the South Pole are both cold places and home to many similar animals, they have very different geographies. The North Pole lies amid a shallow, frozen ocean surrounded by the northern edges of Europe, Asia, and North America. The whole area is called the Arctic (from the Greek *arktos,* meaning bear) because the star constellation called the Great Bear dominates the northern polar skies.

THE ARCTIC

The Arctic region (*above*) consists mainly of the Arctic Ocean, which in places measures as much as 1,000 miles (1,600 km) across and has a thin skin of ice on top. The largest island in the Arctic Ocean is Greenland, which is covered by a thick ice sheet. Also part of the Arctic is a band of land called the tundra, which means "treeless land." This covers the northern parts of Canada, Alaska, Russia, and Scandinavia. On maps, an imaginary line called the Arctic Circle surrounds the Arctic area.

LIVING IN THE ARCTIC

Polar bears (*right*) are the only animals to live and hunt on top of the Arctic Ocean – polar bear tracks have been found even near the North Pole. Probably about twenty thousand to twenty-five thousand polar bears are wandering alone over the remote Arctic ice floes, hunting for seals beneath the ice.

ARCTIC FLOWERS

The tundra landscape (*left*) is generally low and flat, with no trees but many low bushes, lichens, mosses, and grasses. In summer, parts of the tundra burst into bloom as flowering plants rush to flower and produce seeds before the short spell of warm weather ends. There are over 500 species of flowering plants in the Arctic.

THE ARCTIC ICE

The middle of the Arctic is frozen year-round, although the ice is usually less than 30 feet (10 meters) thick.

In winter, the ice covers an area 1½ times the size of Canada, but the edges melt in summer.

The seabed is a pitch-black world of underwater mountains, ranges of hills, and vast, flat plains.

NORTH AMERICA

ASIA

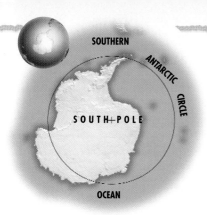

SOUTHERN

ANTARCTIC

CIRCLE

SOUTH POLE

OCEAN

THE SOUTH POLE

The South Pole lies on the continent of Antarctica – the name means "opposite the Arctic." Antarctica is a mountainous continent that is almost completely covered by a gigantic ice sheet and is the size of Europe and the United States put together. Unlike the Arctic, the Antarctic has very little ice-free land, even in summer. It has no land mammals, and fewer plants and animals than the Arctic.

THE ANTARCTIC

The Antarctic region is separated from the rest of the world by the stormy waters of the Southern Ocean (*above*). In winter, ice extends hundreds of miles out into the ocean from the Antarctic coast. There are several groups of remote islands near Antarctica (such as South Georgia), but the nearest landmass is the southern tip of South America, which is about 600 miles (960 km) away. On maps, the Antarctic region is bordered by an imaginary line called the Antarctic Circle.

ANTARCTIC FLOWERS

Only two flowering plants grow in Antarctica, and neither of them looks much like a flowering plant, because they have tiny, drab-colored flowers. The more common one is Antarctic hairgrass (*right*), and the other is a type of pearlwort called *Colobanthus*.

WINTER IN ANTARCTICA

Penguins live only in the southern half of the world, mainly in and around Antarctica, so polar bears and penguins never meet. Only four species of penguin, among them the Adélie and the emperor, breed on the Antarctic continent itself. Most penguins come ashore to breed during the summer. But the emperor penguin (*right*), however, lays its eggs in the winter which allows the chicks to hatch in early spring and have the whole summer to grow.

ANTARCTIC ICE

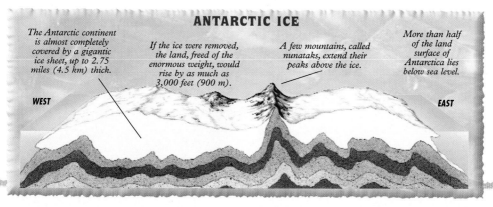

The Antarctic continent is almost completely covered by a gigantic ice sheet, up to 2.75 miles (4.5 km) thick.

If the ice were removed, the land, freed of the enormous weight, would rise by as much as 3,000 feet (900 m).

A few mountains, called nunataks, extend their peaks above the ice.

More than half of the land surface of Antarctica lies below sea level.

WEST

EAST

POLAR PLANTS

It is amazing that any plants at all survive in polar lands, considering the short summers, thin soils, searing cold winds, and lack of moisture. In the Arctic the soil is permanently frozen below the surface but the top layer thaws in summer. Water cannot drain away, so the waterlogged summer soil is boggy and marshy with many lakes and ponds. Arctic plants have to cope with these wet soils as well as the cold and dry air. They tend to grow close to the ground, clustering in tussocks, cushions, carpets, and rosettes, in order to keep out of the wind, to trap moisture, and to avoid being crushed by snow and ice. The leaves of polar plants are often thick and waxy and have few breathing holes, in order to keep water from escaping.

MEAT-EATING PLANTS

Sundews gain extra nutrients by trapping insects with their sticky flypaper-like leaves (*above*). The leaves are covered with special hairs that have drops of glue on the ends. Any insect attracted to the glistening drops is likely to become trapped on the sticky hairs. The leaf then slowly curls around the insect's body, and the hairs pour out digestive juices that turn the body into a soupy pulp. The plant absorbs its insect soup, and after a day or so all that is left of the insect is a dry, empty husk.

ARCTIC WILLOW

Although there are no tall trees on the tundra, the remarkable Arctic willow (*right*) manages to survive by creeping along the surface. Its branches ordinarily do not rise more than 10 inches (25 centimeters) from the ground, but they may be more than 16 feet (5 m) long. The Arctic willow's shoots and leaves have more vitamin C than an orange.

ARCTIC POPPY

The bowl-shaped flowers of the Arctic poppy (*right*) work like a reflecting dish to focus the Sun's rays onto the central part of the flower. In addition, the flower turns to follow the path of the Sun. Both these adaptations help keep the seeds warm so they will develop quickly before the summer Sun disappears from the sky. Arctic poppies grow in low cushions, like many polar plants.

POLLINATION

The hairy "fur" on a bumblebee (*left*) helps it keep warm, but few insects survive in the far north. Most Arctic plants cannot rely on insects to spread their pollen so that their seeds can grow. Instead, the pollen is spread from plant to plant by strong winds. Many plants reproduce in a different way: they grow new pieces of themselves, such as small bulbs or creeping stems called runners.

TUNDRA PLANTS

Colorful, flower-filled meadows (*above*) appear on the Arctic tundra in the short northern summer. Some of the flowers produce their seeds inside berries, such as bilberries, cranberries, bunchberries, raspberries, and crowberries. Many Arctic plants, such as bilberries, are self-pollinating – that is, they use their own pollen to produce seeds. Self-pollination means they do not have to rely on the wind or insects to spread pollen. The new plants that grow from the seeds are identical to their parent plants.

FROM FLOWER TO SEED

Since the Arctic summer is so short, plants such as this purple saxifrage (*left*) must produce their seeds and ripen them in one season. The seeds must be ready to sprout or germinate as soon as possible the following summer. They spend the winter resting in the soil, waiting for the warmth and moisture they need to trigger germination.

ANCIENT LICHENS

In both polar regions the most successful species among plantlike organisms are mosses, algae, and lichens (*left*). The Antarctic has over 400 types of lichens (actually a combination of a fungus with algae or cyanobacteria). Some are thousands of years old but are still very small because growth is slow in the cold.

PLANT EATERS

The leaves, shoots, roots, and berries of tundra plants provide food for a variety of animals, including this brown bear (*right*). Bears eat as much as possible in the summer to build up a store of fat to last them through the winter. There is even a berry called a bearberry, of which bears are said to be fond.

ARCTIC ANIMALS

SEALS

The most numerous and widespread seal resident in the Arctic is the ringed seal, which may even appear at the North Pole. The other main Arctic seals, the harp seal (*above*) and the hooded seal, are migrants. Some harp seals travel about 2,000 miles (3,500 km) to give birth on Arctic ice floes in late winter. By the time the seal pups are old enough to hunt on their own, summer has arrived and there are plenty of fish in the sea.

From tiny, buzzing insects and scurrying lemmings to huge caribou (reindeer), polar bears, whales, and walruses, the Arctic and tundra lands are full of a surprising variety of animals, both in the sea and on the land. Many mammals and birds are migrants, moving north in summer from the lands or seas outside the Arctic Circle. These include caribou, ducks, geese, swans, wading birds, and some seals, which visit the Arctic to feed and breed. This means that the number and variety of Arctic animals change dramatically with the seasons. The few hardy permanent Arctic residents include musk oxen, polar bears, some seals and whales, Arctic foxes, and birds such as the ptarmigan and ivory gull. Unlike the Antarctic, there are land birds as well as seabirds. Summer lakes and bogs provide breeding grounds for millions of mosquitoes and other biting insects, while flowering plants on the tundra attract butterflies, bees, and beetles.

LEMMINGS

Tunneling among Arctic plants, rocks, or soils are large numbers of lemmings. These small rodents (*left*) are plant eaters, and they form an important source of food for meat-eating animals such as Arctic foxes, stoats, and owls. Lemmings make ball-shaped nests out of plant material, and females often give birth to the first litter of the year beneath the snow at the end of winter. If there is plenty of food, one female can have as many as eighty-four young in one year.

WALRUSES

Living only in the Arctic, walruses are not seals, but are closely related to them. Both male and female walruses have two long, sharp, curved tusks, which are actually upper canine teeth. In fights, walruses attack each other with their tusks. Walruses use their fleshy noses and whiskers to find clams, crabs, and other shellfish, as well as worms, on the seabed.

THE ARCTIC FRITILLARY BUTTERFLY

The Arctic fritillary (*right*) is one of the few butterflies found within the Arctic Circle and is one of only about six species of butterfly to survive in Greenland. Its dark markings help to absorb warmth from the Sun, and the speckled pattern on its wings camouflages it from enemies, such as birds and spiders.

THE DOVKIE

There are no penguins in the Arctic but dovekies (*left*), or little auks, look a lot like them. The birds have come to look similar because they have adapted to a similar environment. Both birds have a streamlined shape for swimming underwater along with flipperlike wings. The main difference is that the dovekie can fly, but penguins cannot. The little auk is not much bigger than a thrush, but it is very successful at living in the Arctic.

WILD WOLVES

Although wolves (*right*) live in a variety of habitats, they are well adapted to life in the Arctic. Their thick fur keeps them warm, and often turns white for camouflage. This helps them get close to their prey without being seen. Arctic wolves hunt in packs so they can catch large animals such as caribou and young musk oxen. They also eat carrion and small mammals, such as voles, lemmings, and hares. Superb hearing and a keen sense of smell allow a pack of wolves to track down prey. The wolves relentlessly pursue their quarry for long distances without tiring thanks to their strong bodies and long legs.

LIFE IN SLOW MOTION

The cold temperature of the Antarctic water and the scarcity of available food mean that life runs in slow motion and invertebrates (animals without backbones) tend to grow slowly. They live longer and reach larger sizes than species from warmer places.

The seabed around Antarctica is sometimes covered with countless red starfish, some of which can live for nearly 40 years.

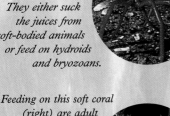

Sea spiders walk or crawl on the ocean floor on their 8, 10, or 12 long legs. They either suck the juices from soft-bodied animals or feed on hydroids and bryozoans.

Feeding on this soft coral (right) are adult isopods, relatives of pill bugs and other wood lice. One giant isopod of the Antarctic can grow as long as 8 inches (20 cm).

ANTARCTIC ANIMALS

There are few ice-free areas of land on the continent of Antarctica, and the largest animal that lives on land all year round is a tiny wingless midge only half an inch (12 mm) long. During the summer, however, the ice around the fringes of the continent melts, and animals such as penguins, seals, and seabirds come ashore to breed. On the islands around the Antarctic continent, the climate is less harsh and the variety of plant life greater – which encourages a greater variety of animal life, particularly birds such as albatrosses and petrels. Sheathbills are the only land birds to live year-round in Antarctica; other birds leave in the winter. Although life on the land is restricted by the ice and the climate, life in the seas around Antarctica is incredibly rich – twice as rich as in the Arctic. Small animals include plankton, corals, anemones, sponges, worms, and starfish, and there are also larger creatures such as fish, seals, and whales.

BLUE WHALE

The Southern Ocean around Antarctica has a greater variety and quantity of whales than any other ocean. They range from toothed whales, such as the killer whale, to baleen whales, such as the blue whale (*right*). Baleen whales filter food through fringes of tough skin (called baleen) that hang down inside their mouths. Blue whales are the largest known animals that have ever lived. Adults weigh more than thirty elephants and are longer than a jumbo jet.

BLUE-EYED SHAGS

The blue-eyed shag (*left*), also known as the imperial shag or cormorant, dives after fish in the ocean. Shags never fish far from their nest or roost sites, and they use their rookeries all year-round. Their rookeries are on remote Antarctic islands and the very northern tip of the Antarctic Peninsula.

TINY KINGS

Mites and springtails (*right*) are the dominant land animals in Antarctica. Mites are related to spiders. Springtails are wingless creatures once thought to be a type of insect. Both have antifreeze in their bodies to keep them from freezing to death. They reproduce when the temperature rises above freezing.

WEDDELL SEAL

Weddell seals (*right*) spend the whole winter under the ice that covers the seas around Antarctica. They make breathing holes in the ice with their teeth and may have to grind through ice many yards thick. If they fail to keep their breathing holes open, they will drown. These hardy seals can dive to depths as great as 2,300 feet (700 m) and stay underwater for more than 80 minutes. They communicate using a series of weird calls that bounce off the ice and carry for many miles underwater.

ADÉLIE PENGUINS

Adélie penguins (*above*) spend the winter out at sea. When they return to their breeding colonies on the Antarctic continent in October, there is still a lot of sea ice between them and their nest sites. They have no time to wait for the ice to melt, so they march inland over the ice for distances of up to 60 miles (100 km).

SURVIVING THE COLD

Animals living in both polar regions have made similar adaptations in order to survive in these hostile environments. Thick layers of fur, feathers, or fatty blubber help keep out the cold and trap the heat given off by the body of a bird or a mammal. Many are forced to migrate to warmer places in the winter, but a few small mammals (such as the Arctic ground squirrel) hibernate over the winter. Icefish and some tiny land creatures survive all year round thanks to antifreeze in their blood. The dark colors of these tiny animals absorb the Sun's heat and help them keep warm.

BLUBBER

The thick blubber of this baby seal (*above*) keeps body heat from escaping. Blubber is a layer of fat under the skin. Whales also rely on blubber for warmth. The blubber can be up to 10 inches (25 cm) or more thick.

Cubs stay with their mother for a year or more to learn how to survive and hunt on their own.

Hairs in the coat are hollow and trap warm air near the body, like double-glazed windows.

Yellow-white fur is useful for camouflage. The color of the fur comes from the way light reflects off the colorless, hollow hairs.

Under the fur, a thick layer of blubber insulates the bear against the cold and acts as a food supply when food is hard to find.

Polar bear hairs are transparent, allowing the Sun's heat to penetrate through the fur to the skin, which is black and absorbs the heat.

BODY WARMTH

When emperor penguin chicks are about eight weeks old, they are too big to hide under their parents for warmth. Instead they huddle together and rely on their dense, fluffy feathers and the warm bodies of their fellow chicks to keep warm (*right*). Conditions are so harsh in the Antarctic that only a small fraction of emperor penguin chicks survive their first year.

ANTIFREEZE

The antifreeze in the blood of icefish keeps ice crystals from forming. In the middle of winter, when the top of the ocean is solid ice, these fish manage to survive in the almost frozen waters below. Fish without this adaptation would freeze to death in these conditions.

SHELTER

Wandering albatross chicks (*right*) sit on the nest for up to a year through winter blizzards and snowstorms. They are protected from the cold by thick down feathers and an insulating layer of fat under the skin. A chick's survival depends on how successful its parents are at finding food in the stormy Southern Ocean.

Small, round ears lose little heat.

POLAR BEARS

The polar bear of the Arctic (*left*) is the largest bear in the world – an adult male can be nearly twice as tall as a person and six times as heavy. Its bulk helps it keep warm, as does its thick fur coat, which is made up of two layers – a thick underfur of short hairs and an outer coat of long guard hairs. The guard hairs stick together when they get wet, forming a waterproof barrier.

A polar bear's nose is just about the only part of the body that is not furry.

Its big paws have rough, furry, nonslip soles to grip slippery snow and ice.

Powerful legs enable a polar bear to walk and swim long distances when hunting prey, although it becomes overheated after running for a long period of time.

ANIMALS ON THE MOVE

Walking and running over slippery ice and soft snow are not easy. Polar mammals and birds often have wide, flat feet with fur or feathers between the toes which spreads out their weight like snowshoes do for humans, and keeps them from sinking into the snow. On slippery slopes some penguins lie down on the snow and slide down like live toboggans. Polar birds that can fly need powerful wings to survive the strong winds and make long migration journeys. They require plenty of food in order to have the energy to fly. Before migrating, they store energy in the form of fat in their bodies, as do the many polar animals that migrate to and from the Arctic and Antarctic every year. The blubber of whales, seals, and penguins is a useful source of energy for their long journeys. The blubber also helps to smooth out their body shape, making them more streamlined so they can swim faster and farther.

PORPOISING PENGUINS

In order to breathe while swimming fast, penguins often leap out of the water (*above*). They travel through the air at speeds of up to 16 miles (25 km) per hour. This technique of leaping in and out of the water is called porpoising. When submerged, penguins use their stiff wings to almost fly through the water. They steer with their feet and tails.

MIGRATION JOURNEYS

Caribou, or reindeer, are always on the move, trekking incredible distances (*left*), in some cases more than 3,000 miles (5,000 km) – the longest journeys of any land mammal on Earth. The animals migrate between forests on the edge of the Arctic, where they shelter in the winter, and the Arctic tundra, where they feed in summer. They follow well-marked trails that are often hundreds of years old and usually cross many fast-flowing rivers. A line of migrating caribou may stretch nearly 200 miles (300 km).

JET SET

Torpedo-shaped squid (*right*) are an ideal shape for shooting through the water fast. They use a method of jet propulsion to accelerate rapidly. By pushing a narrow jet of water out of a funnel at the front end of its body,

the squid shoots off in the other direction, which is backward. The funnel can be curved for swimming forward. Larger squid can swim at up to 20 miles (30 km) per hour – a very useful capability when they need to escape from predators such as sperm whales.

WIDE WINGS

The spectacular wandering albatross (*right*) has the largest wingspan of any bird today – up to 12 feet (3.7 m). It spends most of its life at sea gliding on its huge wings, whose long, narrow shape is ideal for picking up air currents. The bird glides at great speed for long distances, hardly beating its wings at all. It can reach speeds of 55 miles (88 km) per hour and keep going for days at a time.

WHALE TAILS

The flat, rigid flukes (*left*) of a whale's tail move up and down to push the animal forward through the water. Swimming movements are powered by large muscles lying above and below the backbone. About a third of a whale's body is pure muscle. The body's huge bulk is supported by the water pushing up against the animal's skin. The whale's blubber also helps it float.

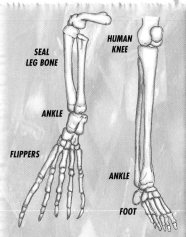

SEAL LEG BONE

HUMAN KNEE

ANKLE

FLIPPERS

ANKLE

FOOT

SEAL FLIPPERS

From the outside, the flipper of a seal looks very different from a human arm or foot. But inside, the bones are the same (*above*). As seals evolved over millions of years, their limbs became webbed paddles, which push them through the water faster than we can swim using our hands and feet. The flipper has a bigger surface without gaps and pushes more water out of the way at each stroke. True seals use their back flippers for swimming; sea lions and fur seals use their front flippers instead.

SNOWSHOE FEET

Arctic hares (*left*) have wide, flat feet with a lot of fur underneath. Their feet help them run or walk over snow without sinking in very far. Their long back legs allow them to bound along quickly, which is vitally important when they are escaping from predators such as Arctic foxes.

ARCTIC FOX

ARCTIC HARE

LEAVES & BERRIES

Land food chains are very different in the Arctic and Antarctic. The Arctic has a lot of land plants for plant eaters such as Arctic hares, which, in turn, are prey to meat eaters like Arctic foxes. The Antarctic has very few plants. A typical food chain might be a plant-eating mite feeding on fungi and being eaten in turn by a meat-eating mite.

PACK POWER

Hunting in packs of up to 20 animals, gray wolves (*above*) range over large areas to find enough food to eat. They can run for many hours, tiring out their prey. Many packs follow migrating herds of caribou, picking off old, young, and sick animals that stray from the main herd. The wolves disable their prey by biting its legs and hindquarters, then kill it with a bite to the throat.

PREDATORS AND PREY

Predators and prey in the Arctic Ocean are remarkably similar to those in the ocean surrounding Antarctica. Killer whales are the top predators in both polar regions. They attack in groups, like wolves on dry land, which allows them to catch and kill bigger animals than they could on their own. Predators are usually strong, fierce animals, with sharp teeth, claws, or beaks to help them catch their prey. They often have to move very fast to catch up with their next meal before it escapes. Food is scarce in polar regions, and predators may go without food for several days at a time.

PATIENT HUNTER

To catch a ringed seal, a polar bear may need to wait patiently for it to come up for air (*left*). Thanks to its white coat the bear blends into the white, snowy background as it keeps still and silent, perhaps for several hours. As soon as the seal comes to the surface, the polar bear pounces, killing its prey with a blow from its huge paws and a bite at the back of the skull. The bear is so powerful, it can drag a seal out of the water through a small hole in ice that is several yards thick.

SEA CATS

Like their spotted namesakes on land, leopard seals are strong, swift, solitary hunters. They hide in the water near penguin colonies, making surprise attacks on penguin chicks learning to swim. Chicks make easy prey because they are not very good at diving, so they have little chance to escape. The leopard seal often plays with its prey for ten minutes or more. Then it beats the dead penguin chick against the surface of the water, stripping the victim's feathers off, and turning the skin inside out to get at the flesh. Leopard seals also eat other seals, squid, fish, and krill.

FIERCE AND FURRY

The wolverine (*left*) is strong for its size and has a powerful, crushing bite. Its large feet allow it to chase prey for up to 40 miles (65 km) before it needs a rest. Once it has made a kill, a wolverine quickly tears the victim's body to pieces, hiding most of the meat to eat later, when food may be hard to find.

ARCTIC PREDATORS

There are more predatory birds in the Arctic than the Antarctic because of the variety of small mammals on tundra lands. Snowy owls (*left*) feed mainly on lemmings and other rodents, swooping down to catch them with strong, curved talons.

SOUTHERN STINKERS

Giant petrels (*left*) are nicknamed stinkers after their unpleasant smell. They are about the size of a vulture and use their powerful hooked beaks to kill penguins, shags, and squid, as well as to tear the meat from seal carcasses.

SLIPPERY MOUTHFUL

Puffins (*below*) have special spines on the tongue and top part of the bill. These help them to catch and hold slippery fish, such as sand eels, and carry them back for their chicks. One puffin can hold up to 60 small fish at a time. Puffins catch their food by diving and chasing their fish prey underwater.

OCEAN FOOD CHAIN

KILLER WHALE

SEAL

SQUID

KRILL

PLANKTON

In polar waters, killer whales are top predators feeding on seals and penguins. Seabirds and squid prey on fish and krill, which eat tiny animals and plants, called plankton, that float in the water.

DEFENSE

SEABIRD COLONIES

By nesting in large colonies on steep, rocky cliffs (*above*), seabirds make it very difficult for predators to reach their chicks and eggs. Birds will dive-bomb predators that get too close and shriek alarm calls to their fellow nesters. Birds that nest in clifftop burrows, such as puffins, are also well hidden from the eyes of their enemies.

Penguins zooming through the water, caribou galloping across the tundra, snow geese flying up out of reach of Arctic foxes . . . one of the best means of defense is to move as fast as possible. There is also safety in numbers. Whether it's a herd of mammals, a flock of birds, or a shoal of fish, members of the group help each other spot danger and may cooperate to drive predators away. Nesting in remote and inaccessible places, such as distant Antarctic islands or steep sea cliffs, also reduces the chances of being attacked. Some prey animals try to avoid being seen by having camouflaged fur or feathers that match their surroundings. But not all prey animals are cowards; some have formidable weapons, such as horns or tusks, and are prepared to stand and fight for their survival.

COLOR CHANGE

Many Arctic animals have different coats in different seasons. In summer, when the snow has melted, the bird grows brown feathers to blend in with rocks, soil, and plants (*left*). In winter, the ptarmigan is white (*right*), so it is hard to see against a snowy landscape.

DANGEROUS NOSE

To warn off enemies or intimidate rivals, male hooded seals (*right*) can inflate an extraordinary structure on their nose. This hood is an enlargement of the nose cavity and can be inflated to form a vast sac about twice the size of a football. In addition to the hood, male hooded seals can also force the lining of one nostril out through the other nostril to form a red balloon. When the seal shakes the balloon from side to side, it makes a loud pinging noise.

BRAVE LEMMINGS

In the winter, lemmings (*left*) are hidden from some of their predators in their tunnels under the snow, although Arctic foxes seem to be able to find them easily and ermines are slim enough to chase lemmings through the tunnels. If lemmings are cornered, they put up a hostile defense. Their brightly patterned fur may serve to warn predators of their aggressive behavior and unpleasant taste.

HORN CIRCLE

Musk oxen (*right*) are the size of ponies and are big and strong enough to have only two real predators – wolves and humans. Their horns are long, curved, and sharply pointed with a solid, horny band across the forehead. Males use their horns to fight for females, but they are also useful for defense. A herd of musk oxen will form a tight circle, with sharp horns facing outward and calves or weaker animals sheltering in the middle. This strategy works well against wolves but is not very successful against people with guns.

HEAD TO HEAD

Although the polar bear (*left*) has the advantage of sheer size, the walrus (*right*) has its tusks to use as weapons against such a predator. Its very thick, leathery skin is also useful against the polar bear's sharp teeth and claws. Walruses are fiercely protective of their young, which could be the reason for this standoff.

COURTSHIP

At the start of the brief summer breeding season, many birds and mammals go through elaborate displays and ritual fights to make sure they find and keep the right partners for mating. Among animals such as caribou, walruses, and elephant seals, rival males fight each other for the right to mate with a group of females. Animals such as musk oxen and wolverines mark their territories with special smelly messages designed to keep out rival males or attract females. Antarctic skuas use their long, loud calls for the same purpose. Courtship displays are usually loud and noisy affairs. They may take a great deal of effort and use up a lot of energy. At the same time, they make the courting animals very obvious to passing predators. The displays, however, are necessary to allow females to find the strongest and fittest males and to test whether the partners are ready and able to mate and care for young.

FENCING UNICORNS

The long tusk of the male narwhal (*above*), a type of Arctic whale, may have given rise to the legend of the unicorn. Tusks were sold in many countries long before people had seen the animal. Only male narwhals have a tusk, which they may use to fight other males. Males are sometimes seen fencing with their tusks on the surface of the sea.

ELEPHANT SEALS

Male elephant seals are up to four times heavier than females and have a huge, swollen nose similar to an elephant's trunk (*right*). In the breeding season, the strongest males guard a group of females for mating. They fight rival males and roar challenges to them through their extraordinary nose, which acts like a loudspeaker. The oldest and biggest males usually win the fights. Males do not eat during the breeding season, since they are constantly on guard on the breeding beaches. The beach masters cannot afford to leave their females in order to catch food in the sea because another male will sneak in and take their place.

PENGUIN RITUALS

The striking golden-yellow neck and ear patches of the king penguin (*right*) are used to attract a partner during courtship. As with other seabirds, the partners need to display together to reinforce pair bonds before they can mate.

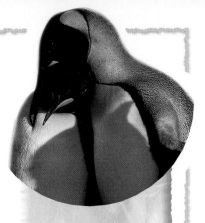

CARIBOU

Male, or bull, caribou use their antlers during the autumn rut, or mating season (*left*). They engage in contests where they clash their antlers together or have neck-wrestling matches with their antlers locked together. These battles decide which of the bulls are strongest and best able to gather, and keep, a small group of cows safe from challenges by other bulls. After the rutting season, the bulls shed their antlers and grow new antlers for the next breeding season.

A pair of king penguins display their brightly colored necks.

Crested penguins swing their heads in a wide arc.

WANDERING ALBATROSSES

These magnificent birds (*right*) live for up to 80 years and tend to stick with one partner for life. When pairs are forming or newly formed, they take part in a long courtship display, but established pairs do not need much courtship. During the display, the male attracts a female by pointing his beak upward, holding out his wings, and whistling. When a female arrives, the two birds dance face to face. They make a variety of noises, clap their bills together loudly, and fence with their huge, hooked bills. When they have paired up, the birds sit side by side on the nest area, nibbling each other's necks and calling softly.

Adélie penguins bow during pair-bonding.

King penguins have a special "advertising" call.

POLAR BEARS

Polar bear cubs stay with their mother (*above*) for at least a year while she teaches them to hunt and survive in the Arctic. For the first few months she feeds the cubs on her rich milk, which is more than 30 percent fat. At birth the cubs are helpless and tiny – only a few thousandths of their mother's weight. They are well protected from the weather and predators inside a warm snow den, dug by their mother. While she is in the den, the mother polar bear cannot eat and lives off fat stored in her body.

NESTS, EGGS, AND YOUNG

Most polar animals lay their eggs or give birth to their young in the brief summer. Many animals, in fact, visit the polar regions only for breeding. They choose to come to these hostile places because there is plenty of food in summer, as well as more space and fewer predators than in warmer places. Two exceptions to the summer breeding cycle are emperor penguins and polar bears, which both rear their young through the winter months. The richest food in polar regions is in the sea, and many parents have to take turns looking after the young while the other partner goes off to feed. Sometimes parents may leave the young on their own or gathered in group nurseries called crèches.

FEATHER NEST

The female eider duck plucks soft down feathers from her breast and uses them to line her nest. These fluffy feathers trap warm air and help keep the eggs warm so they develop properly (*right*). If the parent birds have to leave the nest, they pull the down feathers over it like a warm comforter. Eider ducks nest on small, remote islands in the Arctic Ocean, but their eggs and young are still in danger from predators, such as gulls and foxes, as well as the weather.

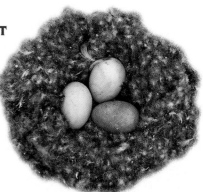

SNOWY OWLS

When there is plenty of food, such as mice, voles, and lemmings, snowy owls may raise seven or eight chicks in one year. If food is scarce, they may not nest at all. The nest is a shallow scrape on the ground, lined with moss or feathers. Owls do not lay all their eggs at once, so there may be chicks of different sizes in the nest (*left*). If there is not enough food to go around, the largest owlet will eat the smallest, then the next smallest, and so on. This seemingly heartless behavior ensures that at least one youngster has a chance of surviving.

SEAL PUPS

Harp seal pups, or whelps, are born on Arctic ice floes, which may last for only a few weeks. The pups need to develop rapidly before the ice disappears, and so they suckle on their mothers' rich milk for only about 12 days (*right*). Their fluffy white coats provide camouflage and help keep them warm. Pups may weigh about 22 pounds (10 kilograms) at birth but add poundage so quickly that they weigh more than three times that when they are only two weeks old. The pups molt and grow their adult coats before following the adults north to the summer feeding grounds. The name harp seal comes from black, harplike markings on the coat of the adult.

EMPEROR PENGUINS

Emperor penguins rear their chicks on the sea ice that forms around the coast of Antarctica in winter (*right*). Emperors do not build nests, but the male keeps the single egg on top of his feet and tucked under a flap. He has to do this for about 65 days without a meal in winds that may reach 180 miles (300 km) per hour and temperatures that may fall below -76°F (-60°C). The female, meanwhile, feeds out at sea. She returns when the egg hatches, and the male struggles to the sea for a well-earned feast. The pair then take turns feeding their chick by coughing up food they have caught at sea.

MOVING BIRTH

Caribou calves (*left*) are born during the migration journey the herds make up to the Arctic tundra for the summer. The calves, plain brown to blend in with the Arctic landscape, are only the size of an Arctic hare at birth. They wobble to their feet within 20 minutes of being born and, by the end of their first day, can run faster than a person. They have to keep up with the rest of the herd, and even tiny calves can cover 9-18 miles (15-30 km) in a day. The calves are vulnerable to attacks by predators, such as eagles and wolves.

LIVING TOGETHER

Living in groups mainly for the breeding season is common for many polar animals such as seabirds, penguins, and some seals. But other polar animals live in groups with an organized social structure year-round, sometimes with a leader that keeps them all together. In these groups, the young stay with their mothers or both parents for a year or more, learning how to survive. Usually only the female young stay in the group, and the males leave to mate with females outside their own family. Relationships between the individuals in a group can be quite complex, with some animals becoming more important than others and each animal having its own place in the group. Group living has many advantages. Group members may help each other find food and stop other animals from stealing it, and may band together to fight predators and protect the young.

KILLER WHALES

Hunting in groups called pods, killer whales (*above*) coordinate their movements by constantly making clicking and calling sounds to each other. The pod hunt like a pack of wolves on land. They attack narwhals, beluga whales, and seals, sometimes tipping seals off ice floes. Group hunting allows killer whales to overcome very large prey, such as blue whales, the largest animals in the world.

CARIBOU

As of 2001, the largest herd of caribou in the world was probably Canada's Leaf River herd, estimated to number over 600,000. A few other herds in North America and Siberia had a few hundred thousand animals, and some smaller herds were thousands strong. For most of the year caribou herds consist of females and their young (*right*). Mature males usually live separately from the females and sometimes move together in compact bands of 100 to 1,000 animals. The only time males and females of all ages come together is during the autumn breeding season. Then the adult males fight to keep a group of 5 to 40 females for mating. The females move freely between groups held by different males, leaving and joining them when they want to.

WOLVES

The body language of the wolves within a pack shows their status or ranking within the group. An alpha, or dominant, wolf (*near left*) will stand erect with its ears and tail pointing upward. It may also show its teeth and growl. A subordinate, or low-ranking, wolf (*far left*) crouches down, turns down its ears, and holds its tail between its legs. Instead of growling, it whines to show it recognizes that the other wolf is superior. Every time one wolf meets another, they use their body language to confirm their status in the group. Only the alpha male and the alpha female in a wolf pack have cubs. The ranking system within a pack helps the group to survive as they cooperate to catch food and rear young in a hostile environment.

MUSK OXEN

A herd of musk oxen (*above*) is made up of females and their young, led by one or more strong males, or bulls. In the mating season, younger bulls are driven out of the herd and form all-male bachelor herds or live on their own. When they grow stronger, they may challenge the master bulls for control. In summer, musk oxen live in herds of about 10 animals, but in winter, the herds join up to form groups of 50 or more.

PEOPLE AT THE POLES

For thousands of years people such as the Inuit of North America and Greenland, the Sami of Scandinavia and Russia, and the Nenets of Siberia have lived in the Arctic. Their bodies have become adapted to tolerate the cold, and they have developed nomadic, or traveling, lifestyles based on hunting wild animals such as caribou, seals, and fish. European explorers, intent on reaching the poles, learned much from the traditional survival skills of these peoples, whose tools, clothing, and means of transportation were perfectly designed for the harsh polar conditions. Today, the Inuit and other Arctic peoples are abandoning their traditional lifestyles. Most have settled in modern homes, go to stores for their food, and work on modern fishing boats or in mines. In the summer, however, some still go out hunting and fishing and combine the old and new ways of life.

ICE SHELTERS

The Inuit igloo, a dome-shaped structure made of snow blocks, was a temporary shelter used on hunting trips. Some Inuit still build igloos for this reason today. The inner walls of an igloo are covered in snow, which melts and freezes into a smooth covering of ice. This igloo (*above*) is lit by a modern kerosene pressure lamp, but light and heat were originally provided by oil lamps burning animal blubber. With the addition of body heat, the igloos keep surprisingly warm inside. In winter, the Inuit traditionally lived in houses made of stone and turf, and in summer they moved into tents made from animal hides.

POLAR TRANSPORTATION

Modern forms of Arctic transportation, such as this snowmobile (*above*), have largely replaced the traditional dogsleds. They are easier to keep than a team of dogs, and their owners can buy fuel and oil instead of having to catch seals to feed the dogs.

INUIT PEOPLES

The Inuit have physical features that help them survive in the Arctic cold. They are short and solidly built, which helps their bodies conserve heat. The thick pads of fat on their cheeks and eyelids protect parts of the body that are exposed to the cold. Their heavy eyelids shield the eyes from the glare of the Sun reflecting off the white snow. Traditional clothing was based on the skins and fur of animals such as caribou, seals, and polar bears. This mother (*left*) is carrying her baby son in a sealskin *amaut*, a sort of hooded parka.

PEOPLE IN THE ANTARCTIC

There are no native inhabitants of the Antarctic, and it was only about 200 years ago that explorers first set foot on the Antarctic continent. Today, many people make scientific expeditions to the Antarctic to study the weather, the wildlife, the ice, and the rocks. Most of them go there just for a few months in summer, although some stay for the winter. This huge dome (*left*) protects some of the buildings of the U.S. Amundsen-Scott base at the South Pole.

REINDEER PEOPLE

This Nenets woman (*below*), from Siberia, is using her domesticated reindeer to pull a large sled full of her belongings. The reindeer have colorful red and yellow blankets and harnesses. Like the Sami people, the Nenets traditionally followed the reindeer herds, eating reindeer meat, milk, and cheese and using reindeer skins for making clothes and for trading in other goods. Today, most have settled in permanent villages.

MODERN PEOPLE

Arctic people traditionally endured some of the most difficult living conditions on Earth by making use of the animals and materials in their frozen environment. Modern technology, however, has transformed their existence (*left*), allowing them to live more comfortably in a world of centrally heated homes, motorized transportation, stores, synthetic clothing, high-tech weapons, and computers. Traditional survival skills are no longer as relevant as they once were.

SAMI PEOPLE

The Sami, or Lapp, people of Scandinavia and Russia (*right*) hunted reindeer from earliest times and used to survive by keeping large herds. They followed the reindeer on their migration, stopping when the herd stopped to feed and sometimes helping the animals across rivers. Some Sami still live in this way today, but the herders' families usually stay in permanent settlements.

PROTECTING THE POLES

The polar regions are important to the survival of the entire Earth. If the polar ice caps melted, fewer of the Sun's rays would be reflected back into space and the Earth's climate would heat up. If the world's oceans get warmer, they will expand, and this, together with the water from the melted ice, would raise sea levels. Also, polar plants and animals belong to a big interconnected web of life that maintains life as we know it. Damage to polar wildlife can affect other parts of the web. Environmental concerns in polar regions include pollution, damage from mining and drilling, and the hunting of endangered species. Today, scientific research has shown how fragile the polar lands are, and laws have been passed to try to minimize damage and protect these unique and extraordinary regions for the future.

MINING

The trans-Alaska oil pipeline (*above*) stretches for 800 miles (1,300 km) from the oil fields of Prudhoe Bay to Valdez, where the oil is pumped into supertankers. The pipeline was built to minimize damage to the environment by avoiding important habitats and the nesting sites of rare birds. It was even raised in some places so that large animals, such as caribou, could migrate underneath. Yet oil spills and damage have occurred.

GLOBAL WARMING

At the moment, the world seems to be getting warmer, causing polar ice to melt (*left*). Many scientists think this global warming may be largely due to a buildup of certain gases in the atmosphere. These gases, especially carbon dioxide, trap heat at the Earth's surface and keep it from escaping into space. To reduce global warming, many people say that pollution and the use of energy should be cut back so that less heat-trapping gas is released into the atmosphere.

HARD TO REACH

The severe weather and difficult terrain of polar regions has helped protect them from exploitation over the years. But today, with advances in transportation and other forms of technology, icebreaker ships can even smash their way through to the North Pole (*right*). The polar regions' wildlife and rich mineral resources, such as coal and oil, act like a magnet, drawing people. Polar resources will become ever more important as those in other parts of the world are depleted.

TOURISM

In the Arctic, tourism is well established and there are wildlife tours and hiking trips. Even in the Antarctic, tourist ships allow their passengers to get really close to seabirds, seals, and whales; some of the wildlife seems very tame (*left*). By visiting these beautiful places, people come to understand the need to protect them. Tourists also bring income and employment to local residents, but they can disturb the habitats and the wildlife they come to see. Their numbers and movements need to be controlled for the sake of the environment.

SCIENTIFIC RESEARCH

Launching weather balloons in the Antarctic (*right*) is just one of many experiments carried out by scientists to help them understand how the polar regions work. Holes that periodically develop above the poles in the atmosphere's protective ozone layer were first discovered over the Antarctic. They seem to be aggravated by artificial gases called CFCs, which have been used in such products as refrigerators and aerosols. The ozone layer is vital because it stops most of the Sun's ultraviolet rays from reaching the Earth's surface. Large doses of these rays can damage living things.

FUTURE FOOD

Krill (*left*) are tiny, shrimplike crustaceans. Most of them are less than 2 inches (5 cm) long, but they are the most important Antarctic animals. They are food for millions of fish, birds, seals, and whales. When whaling bans were introduced to protect endangered species, some fishermen began catching krill, which are rich in protein and vitamins. Ecologically concerned individuals urge that the krill catch be carefully monitored to see how it affects Antarctic animals that depend on krill for survival, just as annual meetings are held to decide how much fish and squid can be caught in the Southern Ocean.

FOR FURTHER INFORMATION

The followng are some of the sources available that can help you find out more about the polar regions and about the protection of polar wildlife.

Books

Anderson, Harry S. *Exploring the Polar Regions* (Facts on File)

Doherty, Craig A., and Katherine M. Doherty. *Arctic Peoples* (Facts on File)

Ganeri, Anita *Protecting Polar Regions* (Gareth Stevens)

Luhr, James F. (editor). *Smithsonian Earth* (DK Publishing)

McGonigal, David, and Lynn Woodworth. *Antarctica: The Blue Continent* (Firefly)

Shirihai, Hadoram, and Brett Jarrett. *The Complete Guide to Antarctic Wildlife: Birds and Marine Mammals of the Antarctic Continent and the Southern Ocean* (Princeton)

Schafer, Kevin. *Penguin Planet* (Creative Publishing)

Soper, Tony, and Dafila Scott. *Antarctica: A Guide to the Wildlife* (Bradt Travel Guides)

Web sites

Antarctic and Southern Ocean Coalition www.asoc.org/

Australian Antarctic Division www.aad.gov.au/

Polar Bears International www.polarbearsinternational.org/

Polar Web arcticcentre.ulapland.fi/polarweb/

70South www.70south.com/resources

U.S. Antarctic Resource Center usarc.usgs.gov/

U.S. National Oceanic and Atmospheric Administration www.arctic.noaa.gov/

WWF www.panda.org/about_wwf/where_we_work/arctic/

Publisher's note to educators and parents: Our editors have carefully reviewed these Web sites to ensure that they are suitable for children. Many Web sites change frequently, however, and we cannot guarantee that a site's future contents will continue to meet our high standards of quality and educational value. Be advised that children should be closely supervised whenever they access the Internet.

Museums and aquariums

American Museum of Natural History
Central Park West at 79th Street
New York, NY 10024

Canadian Museum of Nature
240 McLeod Street
Ottawa, Ontario K2P 2R1
Canada

National Aquarium in Baltimore
501 East Pratt Street
Baltimore, MD 21202

National Museum of Natural History
10th Street and Constitution Avenue, NW
Washington, DC 20560-0166

Peary-MacMillan Arctic Museum
Hubbard Hall
Bowdoin College
Brunswick, Maine 04011

Russian State Museum of Arctic and Antarctic
Marata 24a
191040 St.Petersburg
Russia

Vancouver Aquarium Marine Science Centre
845 Avison Way
Vancouver, British Columbia V6G 3E2
Canada

GLOSSARY

adaptation: an evolutionary change in an organism in response to its environment

algae: a group of simple plants that carry out photosynthesis and range from tiny microorganisms to huge seaweeds; the singular form of *algae* is *alga*

aurora: glimmering lights in the sky of the polar regions caused by the interaction of charged particles from the Sun with the Earth's magnetic field

bacteria: a group of single-celled microorganisms that lack a distinct cell nucleus; the singular form of *bacteria* is *bacterium*

bryozoans: a group of small animals that live in water, usually living together in colonies that may look like moss; they are sometimes called moss animals

CFCs: chlorofluorocarbons – synthetic gases that are thought by many scientists to be harmful to the atmosphere's ozone layer

constellation: a pattern of stars in the sky

cycads: an ancient group of evergreen plants that flourished during the Jurassic period nearly 200 million years ago and is represented today by several tropical species, such as the fern palm.

hydroids: a group of small invertebrates (animals lacking a backbone) that live in water, such as the hydra

lichen: a complex life-form consisting of a fungus plus an organism that can perform photosynthesis – algae or the type of bacteria known as cyanobacteria

ozone layer: a layer of Earth's atmosphere that protects against ultraviolet rays from the Sun; holes in the layer, where much of the ozone is destroyed, have been observed over the polar regions

photosynthesis: a sunlight-based process used by green plants and some microorganisms to make water and carbon dioxide into food

plankton: tiny organisms – including plants, animals, and bacteria – found in a body of water

poles: two points on opposite sides of the Earth through which the planet's axis of rotation passes; located near these geographic poles are two magnetic poles determined by the Earth's magnetic field

pollen: fine grains made by a seed plant that fertilize egg cells, causing them to develop into seeds

predator: an organism that kills other organisms for food

prey: a creature killed for food by a predator

rookery: a nesting or breeding ground for birds

rosette: a circular cluster of leaves

Southern Ocean: the body of water surrounding Antarctica; it comprises areas formerly regarded as the southernmost portions of the Atlantic, Indian, and Pacific oceans

INDEX

A

Adélie penguins 9, 15, 25
albatrosses 14, 17, 19, 25
algae 11
Amundsen-Scott base 31
anemones 14
animals 4, 9, 32, 33
  Antarctic 14, 15
  Arctic 3, 12, 13
  camouflage 13, 22
  courtship 24, 25
  defense 22, 23
  migration 12, 16, 18
  movement 18, 19
  predators, prey 20, 21
  social groups 28, 29
  survival 16, 17
  young 26, 27
  see also named species
Antarctic Circle 9
Antarctic hairgrass 9
antifreeze 15, 16, 17
Arctic Circle 8, 12, 13
Arctic foxes 3, 12, 13, 19, 20, 22
Arctic hares 13, 19, 20
Arctic Ocean 4, 8
Arctic peoples 4, 30, 31
Arctic poppy 10
Arctic seal 12
Arctic tern 5
Arctic willow 10
auroras 7

B

baleen whales 15
bears 11
  see also polar bears
bees 11, 12
beetles 12
beluga whales 28
berries 11
birds 5, 7, 12, 18, 21
  see also named species; seabirds
blue whales 15, 28
bryozoans 14
butterflies 13

C

caribou 7, 12, 13, 30
courtship 24, 25

defense 22
groups 29
movement 18
prey 20
young 27
CFCs 33
climate 4, 5, 6, 7, 32
cormorants 15
cyanobacteria 11

D

dinosaurs 5
dovekies 13

E

eider ducks 26
elephant seals 24
emperor penguins 9, 17, 26, 27
environment 32, 33
ermines 23

F

fish 14, 17, 20, 21
food chains 20, 21

G

global warming 32
gnats 7
grasses 8
Greenland 6, 8, 30

H

harp seals 12, 27
hooded seals 12, 23
huskies 4, 6
hydroids 14

I

ice 4, 5, 8, 9
icefish 16, 17
igloos 30
insects 7, 10, 11, 12
Inuit 30
isopods 14
ivory gull 12

K

killer whales 15, 20, 21, 28
king penguins 25
krill 20, 21, 33

L

Lapp people 31
lemmings 12, 21, 23
leopard seals 20

lichens 8, 11
little auks 13

M

magnetic pole 5, 7
midges 7, 14
mineral resources 32, 33
mites 15, 20
mosquitoes 7, 12
mosses 8, 11
musk oxen 12, 13, 23, 28, 29

N

narwhals 24, 28
Nenets 30, 31
North America 30
North Pole 4, 8
Northern Lights 7

O

oil 32, 33
owls 13, 21, 26
ozone layer 33

P

penguins 9, 13, 14, 15
  courtship 25
  defense 22
  groups 28
  movement 18
  prey 20, 21
  survival 17
  young 26, 27
petrels 14, 21
plankton 14, 21
plants 5, 8, 9, 10, 11
polar bears 8, 9, 12
  predators 20, 22, 23
  survival 16, 17
  young 16, 26
ptarmigan 12, 23
puffins 21, 22

R

reindeer 31
  see also caribou

S

Sami 30, 31
sand eels 21
saxifrage 11
scientific research 31, 33
sea cats 20
sea lions 19
sea spiders 14

seabirds 12, 14, 21, 22, 28, 33
seals 8, 12, 14, 15
  defense 23
  groups 28
  movement 18, 19
  prey 20, 21
  survival 16
  young 27
shags 15, 21
sheathbills 14
shellfish 12
skidoos 30
skuas 24
sledges 30
snow geese 22
snowy owls 21, 26
South Georgia 9
South Pole 4, 9
Southern Lights 7
Southern Ocean 9, 15, 33
sponges 14
springtails 15
squid 19, 20, 21
squirrels 16
starfish 14
stoats 13
sundews 10

T

toboggans 30
tourism 33
transport 4, 30, 33
tundra 8, 11, 12, 21, 27

U

unicorns 24

V

voles 13, 26

W

walruses 12, 23, 24
water 6
weather 6, 7
Weddell seals 15
whales 12, 14, 15, 33
  groups 28
  movement 18, 19
  predators 20, 21, 22
wolverines 21, 24
wolves 13, 20, 23, 29
wood lice 14
worms 14